First Picture Dictionary
Animals

Erstes Bildwörterbuch
Tiere

Pig
Schwein

Rabbit
Kaninchen

Butterfly
Schmetterling

Fox
Fuchs

Illustrated by Anna Ivanir

www.kidkiddos.com
Copyright ©2025 by KidKiddos Books Ltd.
support@kidkiddos.com

All rights reserved. No part of this book may be reproduced in any form or by any electronic or mechanical means, including information storage and retrieval systems, without written permission from the publisher, except in the case of a reviewer, who may quote brief passages embodied in critical articles or in a review.
First edition, 2025

Library and Archives Canada Cataloguing in Publication
First Picture Dictionary - Animals (English German Bilingual edition)
ISBN: 978-1-83416-303-1 paperback
ISBN: 978-1-83416-304-8 hardcover
ISBN: 978-1-83416-302-4 eBook

Wild Animals
Wilde Tiere

Lion
Löwe

Tiger
Tiger

Giraffe
Giraffe

✦ A giraffe is the tallest animal on land.
✦ *Eine Giraffe ist das größte Tier an Land.*

Elephant
Elefant

Monkey
Affe

Wild Animals
Wilde Tiere

Hippopotamus
Nilpferd

Panda
Panda

Fox
Fuchs

Rhino
Nashorn

Deer
Hirsch

Moose
Elch

Wolf
Wolf

✦ A moose is a great swimmer and can dive underwater to eat plants!

✦ *Ein Elch ist ein großartiger Schwimmer und kann unter Wasser tauchen, um Pflanzen zu fressen!*

Squirrel
Eichhörnchen

Koala
Koala

✦ A squirrel hides nuts for winter, but sometimes forgets where it put them!

✦ *Ein Eichhörnchen versteckt Nüsse für den Winter, vergisst aber manchmal, wo es sie versteckt hat!*

Gorilla
Gorilla

Pets
Haustiere

Canary
Kanarienvogel

✦ *A frog can breathe through its skin as well as its lungs!*
✦ *Ein Frosch kann sowohl durch die Haut als auch durch die Lunge atmen!*

Guinea Pig
Meerschweinchen

Frog
Frosch

Hamster
Hamster

Goldfish
Goldfisch

Dog
Hund

◆ *Some parrots can copy words and even laugh like a human!*

◆ *Einige Papageien können Wörter nachsprechen und sogar wie ein Mensch lachen!*

Parrot
Papagei

Cat
Katze

Animals at the Farm
Tiere auf dem Bauernhof

Cow
Kuh

Chicken
Huhn

Duck
Ente

Sheep
Schaf

Horse
Pferd

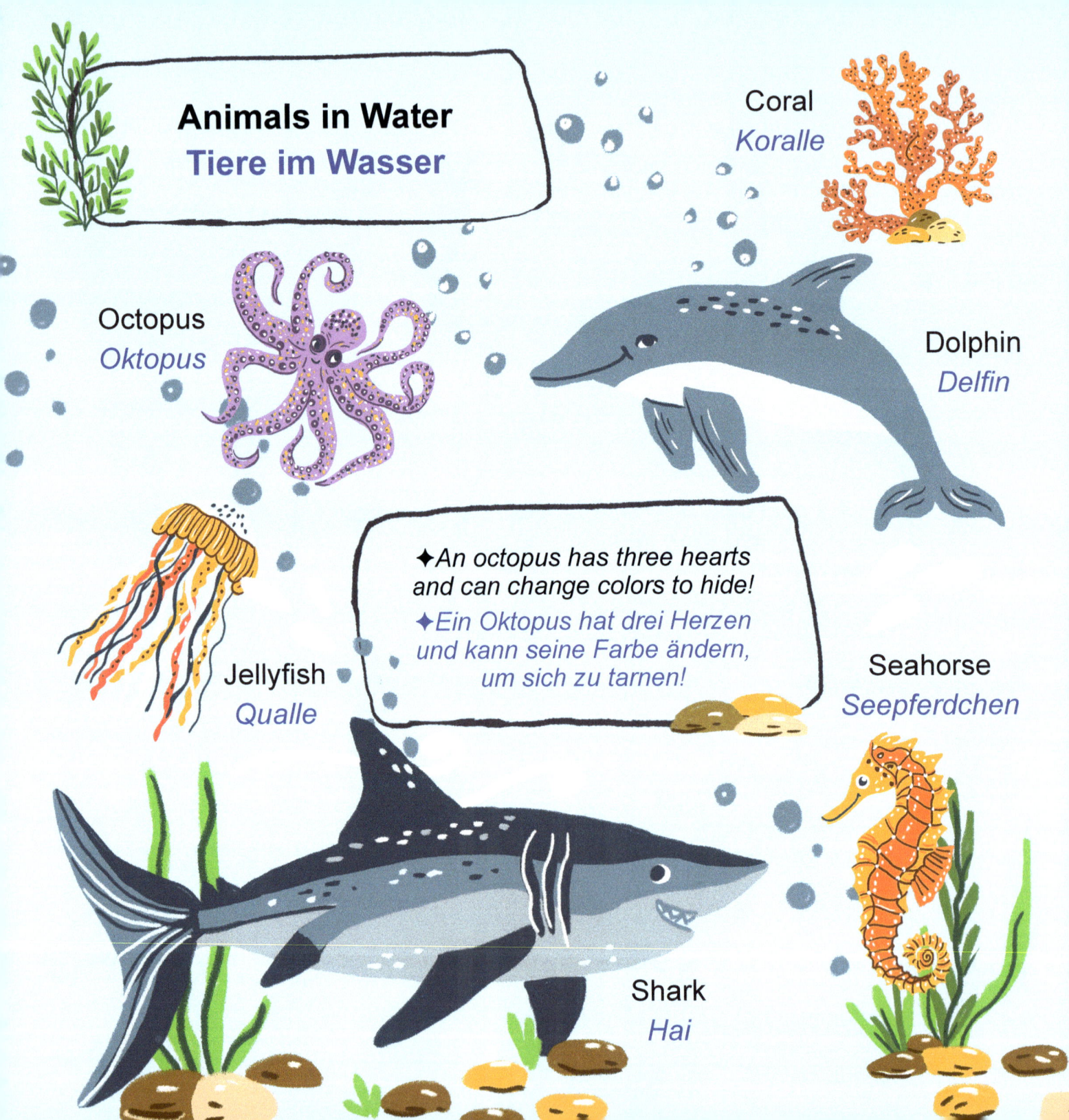

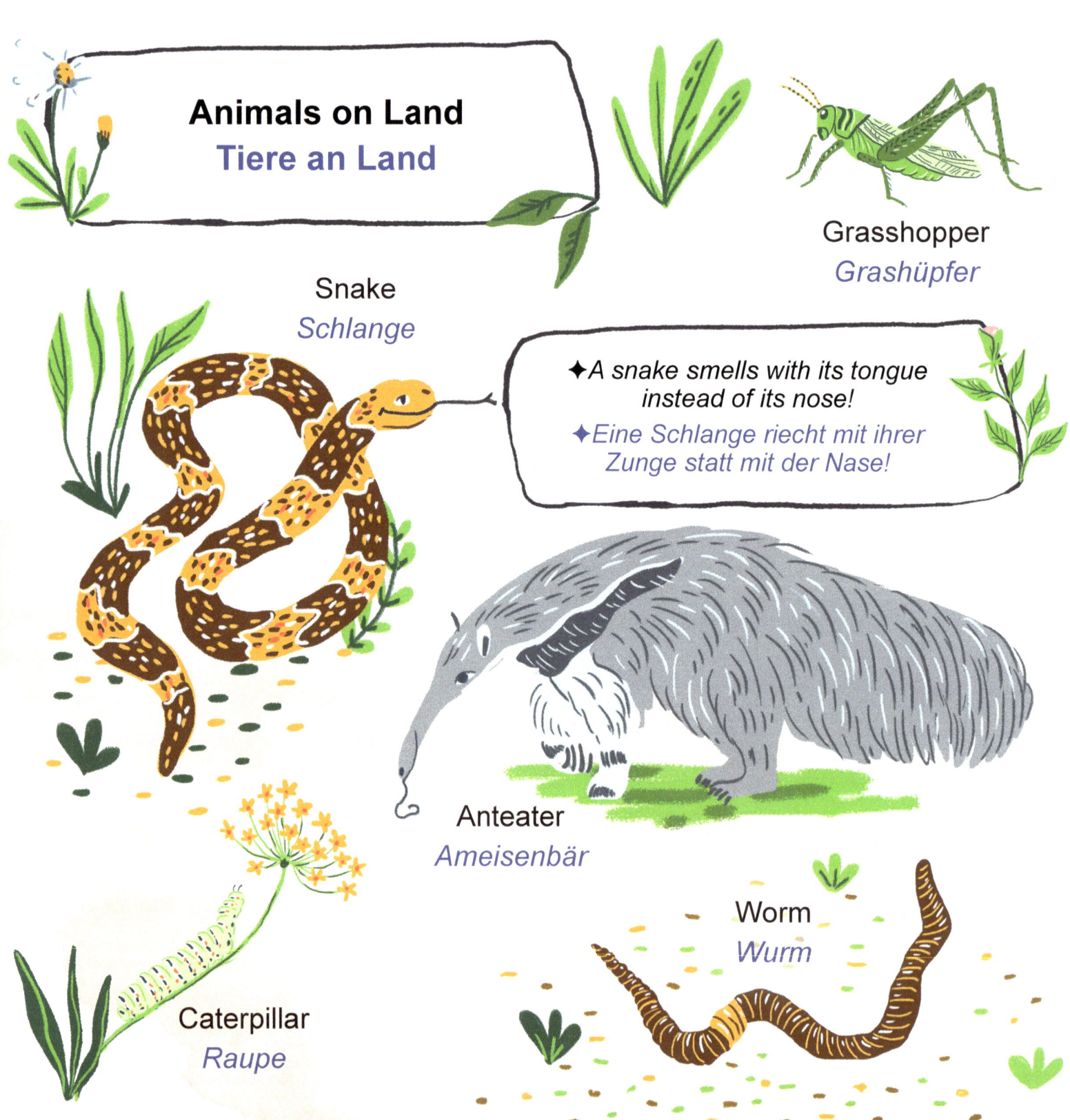

Badger
Dachs

Porcupine
Stachelschwein

Groundhog
Murmeltier

✦A lizard can grow a new tail if it loses one!
  ✦*Eine Eidechse kann einen neuen Schwanz wachsen lassen, wenn sie einen verliert!*

Lizard
Eidechse

Ant
Ameise

Small Animals
Kleine Tiere

Chameleon
Chamäleon

Spider
Spinne

✦ An ostrich is the biggest bird, but it cannot fly!
✦ *Ein Strauß ist der größte Vogel, aber er kann nicht fliegen!*

Bee
Biene

✦ A snail carries its home on its back and moves very slowly.
✦ *Eine Schnecke trägt ihr Haus auf dem Rücken und bewegt sich sehr langsam.*

Snail
Schnecke

Mouse
Maus

Quiet Animals
Ruhige Tiere

Turtle
Schildkröte

Ladybug
Marienkäfer

✦ A turtle can live both on land and in water.
✦ *Eine Schildkröte kann sowohl an Land als auch im Wasser leben.*

Fish
Fisch

Lizard
Eidechse

Owl
Eule

Bat
Fledermaus

✦An owl hunts at night and uses its hearing to find food!
✦*Eine Eule jagt nachts und benutzt ihr Gehör, um Nahrung zu finden!*

✦A firefly glows at night to find other fireflies.
✦*Ein Glühwürmchen leuchtet nachts, um andere Glühwürmchen zu finden.*

Raccoon
Waschbär

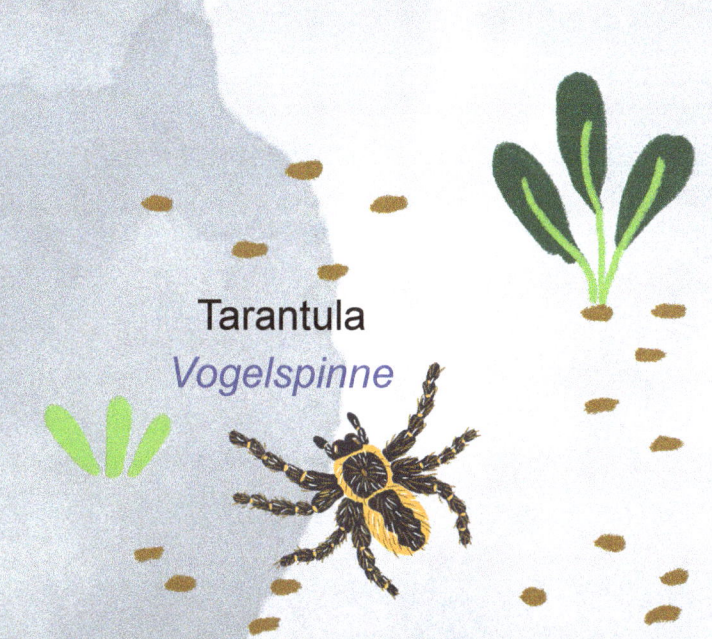

Tarantula
Vogelspinne

Colorful Animals
Bunte Tiere

A flamingo is pink
Ein Flamingo ist rosa

An owl is brown
Eine Eule ist braun

A swan is white
Ein Schwan ist weiß

An octopus is purple
Ein Oktopus ist lila

A frog is green
Ein Frosch ist grün

✦ A frog is green, so it can hide among the leaves.
✦ *Ein Frosch ist grün, damit er sich zwischen den Blättern verstecken kann.*

Animals and Their Babies
Tiere und ihre Jungen

Cow and Calf
Kuh und Kalb

Cat and Kitten
Katze und Kätzchen

✦ A chick talks to its mother even before it hatches.

✦ *Ein Küken spricht schon vor dem Schlüpfen mit seiner Mutter.*

Chicken and Chick
Huhn und Küken

Dog and Puppy
Hund und Welpe

Butterfly and Caterpillar
Schmetterling und Raupe

Sheep and Lamb
Schaf und Lamm

Horse and Foal
Pferd und Fohlen

Pig and Piglet
Schwein und Ferkel

Goat and Kid
Ziege und Zicklein

www.ingramcontent.com/pod-product-compliance
Lightning Source LLC
LaVergne TN
LVHW072056060526
838200LV00061B/4752